anything can ha

anything can happen a poem and essay
by seamus heaney with translations
in support of art for amnesty

FIRST PUBLISHED IN 2004 BY
TownHouse, Dublin, THCH Ltd
Trinity House, Charleston Road
Ranelagh, Dublin 6, Ireland
www.townhouse.ie

Published in association with *Art for Amnesty* and
*Irish Translators' and Interpreters' Association /
Cumann Aistritheoirí agus Teangairí na hÉireann*

PROJECT IDEATOR: Marco Sonzogni
FOREWORD © Bill Shipsey, Amnesty International, 2004
AFTERWORD © Michael J McCann, 2004
DESIGN: Zero-G
COVER IMAGE: Ciarán Ó Gaora

ISBN: 1-86059-235-X

CONTENTS

FOREWORD

To be asked to write a foreword to an essay by Seamus Heaney is a daunting task. Better to say little and invite the reader to turn the page and enjoy his art and the other translations which follow.

The title of the essay, 'Anything can happen', is a modern take on the Latin words *'valet... deus'* in the original version of Horace's Ode. Recent history has unfortunately demonstrated the discomfiting truth of the expression. Whether it be news footage from New York or Baghdad, Madrid or Darfur, we are nightly numbed into accepting that indeed, anything can happen.

Amidst all this gloom Seamus Heaney's essay and adaptation offer hope. It is a hope that Seamus expressed when presenting the first Amnesty International 'Ambassador of Conscience' Award to

Václav Havel. He pointed out that Art for Amnesty 'represents a disposition rather than a party line.' He added 'we are disposed to believe that the work of artists helps to create our future. We believe that the effort of creative individuals can promote a new order of understanding in the common mind, an understanding that precedes and prepares for the establishment of new social and indeed new legislative conditions.'

Art and Human Rights have much in common in that they both offer a blueprint for how we might shape our futures.

Yet again we in Amnesty are indebted to Seamus for giving voice to our aspirations – a very articulate speech of the heart and the head.

Bill Shipsey
Art for Amnesty

ANYTHING CAN HAPPEN

Seamus Heaney

In 1985 the Sandymount Branch of Amnesty International asked me to write a poem to mark that year's Human Rights Day. The poem, entitled 'From the Republic of Conscience', was published by Amnesty as a pamphlet, with artwork by John Behan, and it eventually turned out to be an ongoing if modest contribution to the terms in which the work of the organisation is discussed. It was gratifying, for example, to hear it read last year at the conferral of the first 'Ambassador of Conscience' Award on Václav Havel.

'From the Republic of Conscience' was commissioned but it was not an occasional poem, which is to say it was not a response to some particular occasion. Rather, it was an attempt to give imaginative shape to the overall mission that Amnesty International sets out to fulfil. 'Anything can happen', on the other hand, here published in this special edition in aid of Amnesty, was written in late 2001 in the aftermath of the September 11 attacks, and was first published in *The Irish Times* on 17 November, 2001 as 'Horace and the Thunder'.

In the meantime, through the sustained efforts of members of the Irish branch, Art for Amnesty got itself established and when a reprint of 'Horace and the Thunder' was proposed, to be accompanied by a short essay and several translations, I agreed. Obviously, in the three years since the attacks, there have been terrible consequences, propelling everybody into an increasingly callous and endangered world where 'anything can happen.' Even so, I hope the poem still earns its keep.

ANYTHING CAN HAPPEN
after Horace, Odes 1, 34

Anything can happen. You know how Jupiter
Will mostly wait for clouds to gather head
Before he hurls the lightning? Well, just now
He galloped his thunder-cart and his horses

Across a clear blue sky. It shook the earth
And the clogged underearth, the River Styx,
The winding streams, the Atlantic shore itself.
Anything can happen, the tallest things

Be overturned, those in high places daunted,
Those overlooked regarded. Stropped-beak Fortune
Swoops, making the air gasp, tearing the crest off one,
Setting it down bleeding on the next.

Ground gives. The heavens' weight
Lifts up off Atlas like a kettle lid.
Capstones shift, nothing resettles right.
Smoke furl and boiling ashes darken day.

ANYTHING CAN HAPPEN

HOW EXACTLY art earns its keep in a violent time is a perennial question which has been put in different ways at different periods, from Shakespeare's 'How with this rage shall beauty hold a plea/Whose action is no stronger than a flower?' to Czeslaw Milosz's 'What is poetry that does not save/Nations or people?'

One thing is certain. The indispensable poem always has an element of surprise about it. Even perhaps a touch of the irrational. For both the reader and the writer, it will possess a soothsaying force, as if it were an oracle delivered unexpectedly and irresistibly. It will arrive like a gift from the muse or, if you prefer, the unconscious. It will be like the 'bright bolt' to which Robert Graves once likened the inspiration that came from his own 'white goddess'.

Such a poem arrives from and addresses itself to a place in the psyche that Ted Hughes called 'the place of ultimate suffering and decision', and as nations and people, we have all been driven to the threshold of that place. Acts of coldly premeditated terror, carefully premeditated acts of war, have been experienced by everyone partly as assimilable facts of day-to-day life, partly as some kind of terrible foreboding, as if we were walking in step with ourselves in an immense theatre of dreams.

If poetry has a virtue, it resides in its ability to bring us to our senses about what is going on inside and outside ourselves. As human beings, we crave this realisation and one of the most observable proofs of such craving was the general and urgent quest, in the wake of September 11, for poems that would be equal to that moment. So I was fortunate to remember a work from the past that seemed up to the brutal realities of those days and to the tender mercies they evinced. A work, moreover, that civilians under bombardment might also recognise as some kind of refuge for the mind, if not for the body. One that at least keeps standing its artistic ground even as the rubble keeps falling.

The poem is, in the fullest sense of the term, tremendous. It is about *terra tremens*, the opposite of *terra firma*. About the tremor that runs down to the earth's foundations when thunder is heard and about the tremor of fear that shakes the very being of the individual who hears it.

It was written a little over two thousand years ago by the Roman poet Horace, but it could have been written yesterday in Baghdad. In it, Horace expresses the shock he felt when Jupiter, the thunder-god, drove his chariot across a clear blue sky. Usually, he implies, he would have been ready for thunder and lightning because usually there would have been a massing of clouds and a general threat in the atmosphere. This time, however, the god had arrived so suddenly there was no time to prepare for his terrific sound and fury, and hence it seemed that the safety of the world itself had been put into question.

The poem is in four stanzas, and possesses an uncanny soothsaying force which gives the whole early Roman scenario an eerie contemporary resonance. Not everyone will understand the Latin, but it is still worth quoting:

Parcus deorum cultor et infrequens,
insanientis dum sapientiae
consultus erro, nunc retrorsum
uela dare atque iterare cursus

cogor relictos: namque Diespiter
igni corusco nubila diuidens
plerumque, per purum tonantis
egit equos uolucremque currum,

quo bruta tellus et uaga flumina,
quo Styx et inuisis horrida Taenari
sedes Atlanteusque finis
concutitur. Valet ima summis

mutare et insignem attenuat deus,
obscura promens; hinc apicem rapax
Fortuna cum stridore acuto
sustulit, hic posuisse gaudet.

The following prose translation is a slightly
updated version of a Victorian rendering, yet its old-
fashioned quality is probably useful since it keeps

the poem (for the moment) at a certain cultural and historical distance:

> I have been a reluctant and infrequent wor-
> shipper of the gods, have steered my own
> course and gone with the usual madness, but
> now I am forced back on myself, compelled
> to turn my sails, and retrace the course I had
> forsaken:
>
> For the Father of the sky, who mostly
> cleaves the clouds with a gleaming flash, has
> driven through the undimmed firmament his
> thundering steeds and flying car; whereby the
> ponderous earth and wandering streams are
> rocked, and the Styx and grisly site of hateful
> Taenarus, and the limits of the sea where
> Atlas stands.
>
> To change the highest for the lowest,
> the god has power; he makes mean the man
> of high estate, bringing what is hidden into
> light: Fortune, like a predator, flaps up and
> bears away the crest from one, then sets it
> down with relish on another.

Obviously, there was an uncanny corres-pondence between the words 'valet ima summis mutare... deus' (the god has power to change the highest things to/for the lowest) and the dreamy, deadly images of the Twin Towers of the World Trade Centre being struck and then crumbling out of sight; and there was an equally unnerving fit between the reference to the predatory goddess 'rapax fortuna' and the ominousness of the terrorist attack, since the irruption of death into the Manhattan morning produced not only world-darkening grief for the multitudes of victims' families and friends, but it also had the effect of darkening the future with the prospect of deadly retaliations. Stealth bombers pummelling the fastnesses of Afghanistan, shock and awe loosed from the night skies over Iraq, they all seem part of the deadly fallout from the thunder cart in Horace's clear blue afternoon.

Still, the original is a poem of religious awe rather than any kind of political comment or coded response to events. It is the voice of an individual in shock at what can happen to the world, so the phrase 'anything can happen' would seem to be a fair twenty-first century translation of the Latin '*valet... deus*', in that it expresses the sudden casual desolations of the opening years of our new millennium.

Once I had taken this liberty, I was emboldened to take more and ended up with a version in which the whole first stanza of the Latin was dropped. I even allowed the name Atlas (who stands his etymological ground in 'Atlantic') to prompt a new stanza of my own. But I believe the poem is a fair register of the sense and emotional import of the original, while operating as some kind of answer to what has happened in our own times.

What follows is a series of 23 translations of my adaptation of Horace's Ode, courtesy of the Irish Translators' and Interpreters' Association / Cumann Aistritheoirí agus Teangairí na hÉireann. The adaptation and translations are presented in pairs of what have been termed 'languages of conflict'.

HORACE AND THE THUNDER
after Horace, Odes 1, 34

Anything can happen. You know how Jupiter
Will mostly wait for clouds to gather head
Before he hurls the lightning? Well, just now
He galloped his thunder-cart and his horses

Across a clear blue sky. It shook the earth
And the clogged underearth, the River Styx,
The winding streams, the Atlantic shore itself.
Anything can happen, the tallest things

Be overturned, those in high places daunted,
Those overlooked regarded. Stropped-beak Fortune
Swoops, making the air gasp, tearing the crest off one,
Setting it down bleeding on the next.

Ground gives. The heaven's weight
Lifts up off Atlas like a kettle lid.
Capstones shift, nothing resettles right.
Telluric ash and fire-spore boil away.

Adaptation by Seamus Heaney, 2001

HORÁS AGUS AN TOIRNEACH
de réir Horás, na hÓideanna, 1, 34

Is féidir le rud ar bith tarlú.
Nach eol duit mar is dóichí do Iúpatar
fanacht go mborrfaidh na scamaill
sula dteilgfidh sé an tintreach? Bhuel, anois díreach,
thiomáin sé a charbad toirní agus a eacha ar chosa in airde

trasna spéire glanghoirme. Croitheadh an talamh
agus an domhan pulctha faoi thalamh, Abhainn an Stiocs,
na srutháin lúbacha, cladach an Atlantaigh féin.
Is féidir le rud ar bith tarlú, na nithe is airde

iompú bunoscionn, scáth ar na daoine atá ard sa saol,
meas ar dhaoine gan aird. Tagann Fortún an ghoib
stropáilte anuas de ruathar, ag baint cneada as an aer,
ag sracadh cíor mar spórt, ag ligean dóibh titim áit ar bith.

Tugann an talamh. Éiríonn ualach neimhe
d'Atlás mar a bheadh claibín citil ann,
bogann clocha dín, ní shocraíonn rud ar bith ar ais i gceart.
Fiuchann luaith theallúireach agus spóir thine leo.

Translated into Irish by Micheál Ó Cearúil

UHORACE NEENDUDUMO
Horace, Odes, 1, 34

Izinto ziyenzeka. Ingab'uyamazi na
ugusihamba-ngamafu, utshawuz' imibane
uJupiter? Yiva nangoku, na-a-anko, gqabadu
gqabadu amahash' enqwelo yendudumo

Yasicand' isibhakabhaka sinoxolo. Yaya, ntlithi, ngqu!
Waphethu-phethuk'umhlaba wanikezela,
Zagolokongxo! tshoci kumabhijo-bhij' oMlamb' iStyx,
Unxweme lwe-Atlantika luyayazi loo nto.
Izinto ziyenzeka

Baphequka noorhec' izulu, benesidima nesithozela
 Banikezela banga banengevane,
      Bevuthululwa nguFortune omlom' untshuntshu
Watwabulul' amiphiko wazimk' emoyeni
      Kwaxokozelwa kwabhuduzelwa phantsi kwakhe,
Ebadiliz' ebabhidliza ngathi uyafeketha.
      Babhodloka, bafohloka, bawa le nale naphi na.

Wayekelela umhlaba. Wamthi thwe funqu uAtlas ngamandl' aphezulu
Wanga sisicikwana seketile, kwazama-zama neencopho,
yonk'into yaphelelwa luzinzo, waphenduk' amalahle nomhlaba
kwalephuz' amadangatye.

Translated into Xhosa by Fikiswa Magqashela

HORATIUS EN DIE DONDERWEER
in navolging van Horace, Odes, 1, 34

Enigiets kan gebeur. Jy weet mos hoe Jupiter
wag tot al die donker wolke saampak
voor hy die weerlig werp? Wel, nou-net,
het hy met sy onweerswa en sy perde

deur die blou lug geblits. Die aarde het geskud
en die kluite daaronder, die Styx en
kronkel strome, selfs die Atlantiese kus.
Enigiets kan gebeur, die hoogste dinge

omgekeer, diÈ in hoÎ plekke raak verskrik,
miskendes kry erkenning. Skerpbek Fortuna
laat swiepend die lug na asem snak, ruk
pluime af, wat sy oraloor net vir die pret laat val.

Aardkors gee mee. Die hemel se gewig
lig, soos 'n ketel se deksel, van Atlas af,
megaliet verskuif, niks kom goed tot rus nie.
Aardas en vuurspore bly kook.

Translated into Afrikaans by Sandra Nortje

HORACE DAN HALILINTAR
menurut Horace, Ode 1, 34

Segalanya bisa terjadi. Tahukah engkau Yupiter
selalu menunggu awan bertumpuk,
baru melontarkan halilintarnya?
Baru saja, dia menggelegarkan
kereta halilintar dan kudanya

membelah langit biru yang cerah. Menggoncang bumi
dan dunia bawah bumi yang terbungkam, Sungai Styx,
sungai yang meliuk-liuk, bahkan pantai Atlantik.
Segalanya bisa terjadi, yang tertinggi

ditumbangkan, yang di tempat tinggi nyalinya diciutkan,
yang direndahkan ditinggikan. Fortuna berparuh lancip
menukik, mengaduk udara,
merobek-robek mahkotanya untuk kesenangan,
membiarkannya jatuh ke mana saja.

Bumi menyerah. Beban langit terangkat
dari pundak Atlas, bak tutup ketel,
batu-batu dinding bergeser, semua jatuh kembali berantakan.
Abu bumi dan bibit api menguap habis.

Translated into Basha Indonesian by Teguh Irawan

HORATIUS EN DE DONDER
naar Horatius, Odes, 1, 34

Alles is mogelijk. Je weet hoe Jupiter
gewoonlijk wacht tot wolken kracht verzaam'len
voordat hij bliksem slingert? Wel, zo net
liet hij zijn donderwagen en zijn paarden

langs de helder blauwe lucht gaan. De aarde,
onderwereld, rivier de Styx trilden,
stromen, d'Atlantische kustlijn zelf.
Alles is mogelijk, de grootste dingen

kunnen kantelen, de machtigsten bevreesd,
geringen geacht. Stropvogel Fortuna
duikt en maak lucht ademloos en splijt
heuveltoppen voor de grap en smakt ze neer.

De grond wijkt. Het gewicht des hemels
heft Atlas op, als was 't een keteldeksel,
dekstenen schuiven, niets keert terug naar zijn plaats.
Aardse as en vuursporen verkoken schril.

Translated into Dutch by Arthur Kooyman

הורציוס והרעם

לפי הורציוס, שירי תהילה, 34 ,I

הכול יכול לקרות. אתם הרי יודעים שיופיטר
נוהג להמתין עד שהעננים מתעצמים
טרם הטילו את הברק? אז, זה עתה,
הוא הדהיר את עגלת-הרעם שלו ואת סוסיו

מעבר לשמי תכלת בהירים. זה זעזע את הארץ
ואת הארץ התחתית הסתומה, נהר הסטיקס,
את הנחלים המתפתלים, את החוף האטלנטי עצמו.
הכול יכול לקרות, יכול לקרות שהדברים הגבוהים ביותר

ייהפכו, אלה במקומות רמים יירתעו,
אלה שמעלימים מהם עין ייערכו. הגורל בעל מקור ההשחזה
מסתער, גורם לאוויר להתנשף, קורע
פסגות סתם כך, מטיל אותן לא חשוב היכן.

האדמה זזה. כובד השמיים
מתרומם מעל אטלס כמו מכסה של קומקום,
אבנים עליונות זזות, דבר אינו מסתדר מחדש.
אפר חובק-עולם ונבגי אש רותחים להם.

Translated into Hebrew by Denise Levin

هوراس و الرعد

بعد هوراس ,قصائد غنائية, *34, I*

أي شيء يمكن ان يحدث.انت تعرف كيف جوبي
في الاغلب سوف ينتظر حتى تكتسب الغيوم شدة
قبل ان يقذف الرعد ؟ حسنا , في الحال
يجري بعربة الرعد و الخيل عدوا

عبر سماء زرقاء صافية .زعزعت الارض
و باطن الارض المنسد, نهر أسطقس
الجداول المتعرجة , شاطىء الاطلسي نفسه
أي شيء يمكن ان يحدث , الاشياء الشاهقة

ليسقطوا , اصحاب المناصب العالية مثبطون
اولئك المغفلون يستعيدون اعتبارهم. مصاير المنقار المشحوذ
ينقض, جاعلا الهواء يلهث,متدفقا بعجلة فائقة
رايات للعبث, دعها تتساقط اينما كان

الارض تنهار . السماء تلقي بثقلها
ترتفع عن اطلس كغطاء الغلاية
الحجارة المتوجة تنزاح , لاشيء يستقر كما كان
الرماد التلوري و الابواغ النارية تغلي باستمرار

Translated into Arabic by Raphaël Moussally

ХОРАЦИЈЕ И ГРМЉАВИНА

По Хорацију, Оде, И, *34*

Све је могуће. Знате како би Јупитер
углавном чекао да се облаци прикупе
пре него што завитла муњу? Ево, баш сад,
прогалопирао је са коњима у својим олујним кочијама

преко чистог плавог неба. То је потресло земљу
и зачепљену утробу, реку Стикс,
вијугаве струје, и саме обале Атлантика.
Све је могуће., највишље ствари

да се преокрену, оне с висине да се уплаше,
оне занемарене улију поштовање. Накострешена Судбина
се обрушава, ваздух је у ропцу, откидајући
кациге као од шале, пуштајући их да падну билокуд.

Земља попушта. Небеска тежина
подиже Атласа као поклопац чајника,
крунски камен се премешта, ништа се не поставља на право место.
Земаљска пепео и ватрени заметци испаравају.

Translated into Serbian by Pierre Perković

HORACIJE I GRMLJAVINA
Po Horaciju, Ode, 1, 34

Sve je moguće. Znate kako bi Jupiter
uglavnom čekao da se oblaci prikupe
pre nego što zavitla munju? Evo, baš sad,
progalopirao je sa konjima u svojim olujnim kočijama

preko čistog plavog neba. To je potreslo zemlju
i začepljenu utrobu, reku Stiks,
vijugave struje, i same obale Atlantika.
Sve je moguće., najvišlje stvari

da se preokrenu, one s visine da se uplaše,
one zanemarene uliju poštovanje. Nakostrešena Sudbina
se obrušava, vazduh je u ropcu, otkidajući
kacige kao od šale, puštajući ih da padnu bilokud.

Zemlja popušta. Nebeska težina
podiže Atlasa kao poklopac čajnika,
krunski kamen se premešta, ništa se ne postavlja na pravo mesto.
Zemaljska pepeo i vatreni zametci isparavaju.

Translated into Bosnian by Mikajlo Oklopdzic

HORAZ UND DER DONNER
nach Horaz, Oden, 1, 34

lles ist möglich. Du weißt, wie Jupiter gewöhnlich
abwartet, dass Wolken hoch aufgetürmt sind, bevor
er den Blitzstrahl schleudert? Nun, eben jetzt
sprengten sein Dunnerwagen und seine Rosse

über ei klarblaues Firmament. Es bebte die Erde,
die Untererde, die überfüllte, der Fluss Styx,
die gewundenen Strome, ja, der Rand des Atlantiks.
Alles ist möglich, das Ragendste kann

zu boden gebracht, dei Hochgestellten können geschreckt,
geachtet werden die Unbeachteten. Scharfschnabel Fortuna
stößt herab, lässt die Luft ringen nach Luft, greift
sich Helme zum Spaß, verstreut sie da order dort.

Erdboden sackt. Das Himmelsgewicht
hebt sich von Atlas wie der Deckel vom Topf.
Decksteine verrutschen, nichts kommt wieder ins lot.
Tellurische Asche und Feuersporen brodeln dahin.

Translated into German by Peter Jankowsky

ГОРАЦИИ И ГРОМ

Из Горация, Оды, *1, 34*

Всякое бывает. Знаешь, как ждёт порой
Юпитер тучи грозовой пред тем, как
молнию метнуть? А вот, пустил он колесницу
Громовержца конями запрежённую сквозь

поднебесие прозрачно голубое. Дрогнули земля,
подземелье забитое, Стикс река,
вьющиеся ручьи и брега Атлантики самой.
Всякое бывает: громада может рухнуть,

и верхи быть в страхе, и незамеченный оценен
высоко. Фортуна остроклювая вниз устремляется,
взрывая воздух, срывая ради шутки со шлемов
гребни, регалии роняя эти в никуда.

И поддаётся почва. Тяжесть небес с рук Атласовых
приподнимается как крышка котелка,
смещаются карнизы, ничто не становится как прежде.
Зола земная с искрами огня кипит, кипит.

Translated into Russian by Thom Moore and Lyuba Moore

贺瑞斯与惊雷
和 贺瑞斯之诗集 I, 34

什么事都可能发生。你知道朱庇特
总是等待乌云拢聚之后
才掷出一道道闪电？看哪，就在刚才
他驾着雷电马车疾驰

穿过一片晴空。它震动了大地
以及拥塞的地下世界、冥河、
弯曲的溪流、甚至大西洋海岸。
什么事都可能发生，至高的东西

被推翻，那些身处高位的胆战心惊，
那些被忽视的得到尊重。利喙的幸运之神
呼啸着猝然掠下，自娱地撕掉
肩章顶饰，然后将之随意抛弃。

地裂山崩。天堂的重量
在亚特拉斯的肩头上象烧水壶的盖子一样冲起
顶石移动，万物不再回复平常。
大地的灰烬和星星火种沸腾飞扬。

Translated into Chinese by Li Xuemei

ཉི་རེ་སེ་དང་འབྲུག་སྒྲ། །

ཚོམ་པ་པོ་ཆི་རེ་སེ་སྐྱེན་ཚོམ་གྱུ་དབྱངས་ཤེ་ལོ།

༡ གང་རུང་འབྲུང་བ་ཡིས། ཁྱེད་ཀྱི་རྟོགས། ཧྲ་ཏ་ཏར་གྱིས་ཕོག་བཞུགལ་པ་འབང་སྲ་རོ་ལ་དུ་སྙིན་ཚོག །མང་ཚེ་བ་དང་སྐྲག་མི་བྱེད་དས། །ལེགས་སོ། ད་ལྟ་རང་ཁོ་ལ་རུ་རྣམས་དང་འབྲུག་སྒྲའི་ཤེང་རུ་མཚོང་རྒྱ།

༢ དངས་པའི་དགུང་སྙིན་ཞིག་གི་སྟུ་རོ་ལ་དུ། དེས་སྟེང་ས་གནའི་དགུགས་ས་ཕོག་སྒྱོག །ཤེང་བ་ཅིང་ས། །ཤེ་གཅང་པོ། སར་ཏ་ཡེས་དང་གཙུག་སྐྱིམ་རྒྱ་ཕུན་ཡེ་ཏ་ལུན་ཏེག་རྒྱ་མཆོའི་རོངས་ཀྱུ་བཅིང་ས། གང་རུང་དཔངས་མཐོ་ཤེས།

༣ དརོས་རྫས་མགོ་རྗེ་སྒྲོག །མཐོ་བའི་གནས་སའི་གོ་རེ་མ་དེ་དག་དཔལ་བའི་གཉུལ་བར་གཤོག་སྟྲང་རྒྱང་བརྒྱ་མཐོ་སུ་དུད་བྱས། །བཤོད་ཚམས་ལྕུའི་བུ་རོག་གི་གཟུགས་སུ་བྱས། བར་སྟྲང་རུང་ཁམས་དངས་སུ་ཕམས་ཅད་ཕོག་གཏིབ་རྒྱ། རང་གར་སྒོག་ཆགས་དེ་དག་ས་གས་ནང་དུ་བཅའ་གྱིས་འཕངས།

༤ ས་གནའི་ཡོངས་སུ་གས། ཨེ་ཏ་ལ་སེ་ཡེས། །ལྕུའི་ཞིང་ཁམས་ཕྲེང་ཚོན་ཁོག་ཕྲེར་ཞིབས་གཏོང་ལྟ་བུར་ས་གནའི་གས་དེ་དུ་ལ་རྒྱ་ལྕུགས་ཕྱེ་དང་ཤེ་ལྟ་བུར་བར་སྟྲང་འཁར་ཏེ་ས་གནའི་དེ་དག་ཤེ་ཡི་རྒྱལ་རྒྱ་དེ་དག་སྟུར་བཞིན་འབབབ་ཕྲེང་འཐགས་སུ་མ་གནས།

*
མཆན
༡ ཧྲ་པི་ཏར། རོ་མན་གྱིས་བསྐྱེན་པའི་གཙོ་བོ་ཞིག
༢ དེས། འབྲུག་སྐྱེའི་ཤེང་ང་།
༣ ས་ཏ་ཡེས། (Styx) = རིག་ལུ་སྒྲར་དུ་གྱགས་པའི་གཙང་རོ་ཞིག
༤ ཨེ་ཏ་སེ། (Atlas) = རིག་ལུ་སྒྲར་དུ་གྱགས་པའི་ག་བ་འདེགས་པའི་གཏོན་སྙིན་ཞིག

Translated into Tibetan by Dhonden Tsering

ホレスと豪雷
(ホレスに捧げる叙情詩、オード、I、I, 34)

何が起きたって不思議じゃないんだ。
全能の神ジュピターは稲妻を落としたくて、
いつも嵐雲が湧き起こるのを待っているだろう?
今さっき、二輪の豪雷馬車を轟かせて···

ものすごい勢いで青空を横切って行ったよ。
大地が、閉塞した 雄々しく聳え立っているものだって···
曲がりくねった小川も、大西洋の沿岸まで揺れ動いた。
そうさ、何が起きたって不思議じゃないんだ。
雄々しく聳え立っているものだって···

いつかは引っくり返る。誇り気高い者も、いつか鼻を挫かれる。
気にも留めていなかったことが、本当は掛替えのないものだと
わかる。突然、鋭い嘴で突付かれたように、どこからともなく
さっと舞い降りて来た運命に息を呑む暇もなく、
面白半分に引き裂かれて、ところ構わず置き去りにされる。

大地が屈する時。天がまるでヤカンの蓋を取るように
軽々と大地から離れてしまう。冠石が転げ落ちる。
全てが宙に浮いたまま、再び鎮まることを知らない。
大地の灰と炎の胞子が、唯ただ燻っているばかり。

Translated into Japanese by Naomi Ishikawa Summers

HORACE DAN GURUH
sesudah Horace, Oda, 1, 34

Apa-apa boleh terjadi. Anda kan tahu betapa Jupiter
Akan selalu menunggu mega menghitamkan angkasa
Sebelum halilintar mahu dilontar? Maka baru seketika,
Dia menunggang pedati guruh pacuan gerombolan kuda

Melintasi angkasa bening kebiruan. Bumi bergegar
Jua Sungai Styx yang kian terhambat, tak lagi lancar,
Liku-liku anak sungai, pantai Atlantik pun turut bergetar.
Apa-apa boleh terjadi, yang tertinggi boleh tersasar

Lalu bergelimpangan, menjerankan yang di mercu juga,
Yang tak diendahkan dihormati. Paruh Nasib tajam berbisa
Menjunam dalam kegugupan udara lalu dirabak olehnya
Gencana, dalam suka-suka, berhamburan segalanya.

Bumi pun mengalah. Beban iaitu syurga di pundaknya
Bertunjangkan Atlas ia pun terangkat maka cerek terbuka,
Beranjak mercu dan puncak, tak kembali ke sedia kala.
Jagat jadi abu dan baka pawaka bersemarak menyala.

Translated into Malay by Abd Latiff Bidin

HORACE ET LE TONNERRE
Inspiré de Horace, Odes 1, 34

Tout peut arriver. Souviens-toi de Jupiter
Attendant patiemment que les nuages se regroupent
pour violemment jeter ses éclairs? Regarde, il vient de
passer au grand galop, sur son char de feu, ses chevaux

déchirant le grand ciel bleu. La terre a tremblé,
et le monde des ténèbres, et le Styx,
et les ruisseaux, les côtes même de l'Atlantique.
Tout peut arriver. Les structures les plus élevées

renversées, les personnes les plus haut placées terrifiées,
les oubliés reconnus. Fortune au bec crochu
fond sur le sol, déchirant l'air stupéfié, déchiquetant
Tous les trophées, s'amusant à les laisser s'éparpiller.

La terre s'ouvre. Le poids des cieux
soulève Atlas comme un couvercle,
les dalles basculent, rien ne se remet en place.
Cendres telluriques et bouches de feu gargouillent.

Translated into French by Christelle Petite and Jean-Philippe Imbert

HORACE NA RADI

Baada ya Horace Odes, 1, 34

Chochote chaweza kutokea. Wajua Jupita anavyosubiri mawingo
kujiunga kitambo, kabla ya kuwavurumishia umeme?
Sawa, sasa hivi, ameimeza rukwama la radi pamoja na farasi wake katika
anga iliyokuwa wazi ya samawati.

Hilo limeitetemesha ardhi hata kiini chake kilichozibika, mto Staiksi,
vijito vilivyojipinda, na hata ufuo wa bahari ya Atlantiki wenyewe.
Chochote chaweza kufanyika, vilivyo virefu vikapinduliwa,
vilivyotukuzwa vikadunishwa na vilivyo dunishwa vikatukuzwa.

Bahati hubadilishanwa ghafla, na kusababisha kutweta kwa hewa,
kupasua kilele cha burdani, na kuviachilia vianguke kokote kule
kihotelahotela.

Ardhi husalimu amri. Mbingu huinua Atlasi kama kifuniko cha birika,
vizibo vya mawe hutingizika, hakuna chochote kinachotulia vilivyo.
Majivu na kiini cha moto uliovuma husagaa na kuenea.

Translated into Swahili by Caroline Shiro

HORACIO Y EL TRUENO
de Horacio, Odas, 1, 34

De todo puede suceder. ¿Ya sabéis cómo Jupiter
espera a que se acumulen las nubes
antes de lanzar el rayo? Pues ahora mismo pasó
al galope con su carro estruendoso y sus caballos

por un limpio cielo azul. Estremeció la tierra
y el infierno recargado, el río Estigia,
los arroyos serpenteantes, la orilla misma del Atlántico.
De todo puede suceder, las cosas más altas

pueden volcarse, los que dominan amedrentarse,
los ignorados ser exaltados. La Suerte pico-aguda
cala, ahogando al aire, arrancando
escudos por placer, dejándolos caer al azar.

El suelo cede. A Atlas se le quita de encima
el peso del cielo como la tapadera de una olla,
se desplaza el remate de los muros, nada vuelve a su lugar.
Hierven ceniza telúrica y esporas de fuego.

Translated into Spanish by Anamaría Crowe Serrano

HORAZIO ET A TURMOIA
Horazio, Odak, 1, 34

Denetik gerta daiteke. Badakizue Jupiterrek
oinaztarria jaurti aurretik lainoak pilatu arte
itxaron egiten duela? Bada, oraintxe pasatu da
arrapaladan bere gurdi zalapartatsu eta zaldiekin

zeru ezinago urdinagotik. Dardarka jarri ditu lurra
eta infernu beteegia, Estigia ibaia,
bihurka doazen errekak, Atlantikoaren bazterra bera.
Denetik gerta daiteke, irauli egin daitezke

gauzarik garaienak, menderatzaileak kikildu,
ahantziak goretsiak izan daitezke. Zori erpin zorrotza
sartu egiten da, airea itoaz, plazerraren plazerraz
ezkutuak erauziaz, halabeharrez erortzen utziaz.

Lurrak amore ematen du. Zeruaren zama
gainetik kentzen zaio Atlasari, eltze baten estalkia bailitzan,
hormen errematea mugitu egiten da, ezer ez da bere lekura itzultzen.
Irakiten daude errauts telurikoa eta suzko esporak.

Translated into Basque by Lourdes Auzmendi

होरेस और र्गजना
होरेस के बाद ओदे *1, 34*

कुछ भी हो सकता है, कैसे वृहस्पति अपनी
दामिनी दमकाने से पूर्व, बादलों के एकत्रित
होने की प्रतीक्षा करता है ? हाँ , बस अभी
ही उसने अपने रथ और घोड़ों को दौड़ाया है

नीले आसमान के सामने उसने पृथ्वी, पाताल,
कल कल करती धाराओं और अटलांटिक को
हिलाया है, कुछ भी हो सकता है, विशाल से
विशाल, ज्वलन्त से ज्वलन्त.

वह जो शीर्ष पर बैठे – डरे हुये, नहीं देखा
जिन्होने सफलता को चूमते हुये, हवा को थमते
हुये, खेल के लिये चोटियों को सपाट करते हुये,
बदलो, उठो.

स्वर्ग का भार, केतली के ढक्कन की तरह,
वसुंधरा को उठा दे शहतीरें सरका दे,
कालिख छुपा दे, आग उड़ा दे

Translated into Hindi by a well wisher

ہورس اور تھنڈر
ہورس کی نظم 34 ,I کی تقلید میں

کچھ بھی ہو سکتا ہے ۔ تمہیں معلوم ہے کہ کیسے رومی دیوتا جو پٹر
بجلی گرانے سے پہلے اکثر بادلوں کے جمع ہونے کا انتظار کرتا ہے؟
ہاں ، ابھی ابھی اُس نے اپنے طوفانی چھکڑے اور گھوڑوں کو
شفاف نیلے آسمان پر سر پٹ دوڑایا ہے ۔

اس نے ہلا دیا ہے دھرتی کو اور اس کے اندر جمع چیزوں کو
مردوں کے دریا کو (دریائے سٹکس) ، بل کھاتی ندیوں کو اور ساحل بحر او قیانوس کو بھی ۔
کچھ بھی ہو سکتا ہے ۔

بلند ترین چیزیں الٹ سکتی ہیں ، اونچے عہدے داروں کو پست ہمت کیا جا سکتا ہے
نظر انداز کیے جانے والوں کی توقیر ہو سکتی ہے ۔
تیز چونچ والا عقاب جھپٹتا ہے ، ہر ایک کو حیران کر تا ہوا
کلغیاں اور تاج تفریح کے لیے نوچ کر انہیں ہر طرف بکھیر دیتا ہے ۔

زمین دھنستی ہے ۔
اطلس دیو کے سر اور ہاتھوں سے فلک کا وزن کیتلی کے ڈھکنے کی مانند اوپر اٹھتا ہے ۔
تقدیریں بدلتی ہیں ، کچھ بھی دوبارہ ٹھیک طرح بحال نہیں ہوتا ۔
کرہ ارض کی خاک اور آتشی گولے بھاپ بن کر اڑتے ہیں ۔

Translated into Urdu by Sohail Raza

HORACE VE GÖKGÜRÜLTÜSÜ
Horace, Odes, 1, 34 'e atfen

Her şey olabilir. Tanrılar Kralı Jupiter'in
şimşekleri savurmadan önce nasıl çoğunlukla bulutların
toplanmaşını bekledigini bilir misin? Evet, şimdi,
gökgürültüsü arabasını ve atlarını dörtnala

masmavi gökyüzünde yola çıkardı. Yer sarsıldı
ve üzerine ayakların bastığı yeraltı ile Styx ölülüler nehri,
sarmal dereler, hatta Atlantik kıyıları sallandı.
Her şey olabilir, en yüksek şeyler

devrilebilir, yüksek yerlerdekiler yılabilir,
tepeden bakılanlar itibar kazanabilir. Keskin gagalı Talih kuşu
havayı soluklandırıp, eğlence olsun diye başlıkları
gagasıyla kapıp her yere saçabilir.

Yeryüzü verir. Göklerin ağırlığı
Atlas'ı su ısıtıcısının kapağı gibi kaldırabilir,
kapaktaşları yerinden oynayıp, her şey allak-bullak olabilir.
Yer külleri ve ateş hücreleri kaynar.

Translated into Turkish by Ali Murat Yel

Ο ΟΡΑΤΙΟΣ ΚΑΙ Ο ΚΕΡΑΥΝΟΣ

κατά Οράτιο, Ωδές, *1, 34*

Όλα μπορούν να συμβούν. Ξέρεις πως ο Δίας
περιμένει πρώτα να ωριμάσουν τα σύννεφα
πριν εξαπολύσει τις αστραπές του; Ιδού, μόλις τώρα,
καλπάζοντας με το βροντώδες άρμα του και τ' άλογά του

διάβηκε τον καταγάλανο ουρανό. Σείστηκαν η γη
κι ο κατάφορτος Άδης, τα ύδατα της Στυγός,
τα φιδωτά ρυάκια, του Ατλαντικού οι ίδιες οι ακτές.
Όλα μπορούν να συμβούν, τα πιο απίθανα πράγματα

ανατροπές, φοβέρες για τους έχοντες αξιώματα υψηλά,
τιμές για τους καταφρονεμένους. Η γαμψώνυχη Μοίρα
εφορμά, κάνοντας τον αγέρα να στενάζει, ξηλώνει
βουνοκορφές για κέφι κι ολούθε τις σπέρνει.

Το έδαφος υποχωρεί. Τ' ουρανού το βάρος
εξακοντίζεται άξαφνα πάνω απ' τον Άτλαντα,
κορωνίδες μετατοπίζονται, τίποτα πια δε γαληνεύει.
Τελλούρια σποδιά και σπόροι φωτιάς σιγοκαίνε.

Translated into modern Greek by Panos Kiliorides

A poet, in translation, with something to say

Quintus Horatius Flaccus, known as Horace in English, was a poet whose life spanned some of the most tempestuous years of Roman history. He fought in the civil wars which followed the assassination of Julius Caesar, witnessed the triumph of the Emperor Augustus and died eight years before birth of Christ. His poetry survived, and became, as he predicted it would, 'more enduring than bronze'. It records one man's effort to maintain sanity and balance in times of the greatest turmoil and upheaval.

Seamus Heaney's adaptation of one of the Odes, which immortalised this Roman poet, is as gripping in English as the original Latin. Here, in 23 languages, is the translation of that version, in what we have termed the 'languages of conflict'.

The Irish Translators' and Interpreters' Association / Cumann Aistritheoirí agus Teangairí na hÉireann is delighted to co-operate with Amnesty International in assembling these new versions. Our mutual interest in fostering open exchanges between peoples is well served by such an enterprise, and the ITIA was in a position to provide access directly or through its members to skilled professionals.

Conflict can arise due to the inability to speak another language. That unlearned language may not just be a barrier to communication, but can give rise to a constant danger of international misunderstanding.

Translators, like the poets of yesteryear and today, are but one voice for mutual understanding. But like the poets, they remain an essential voice.

Michael J McCann
Chairman ITIA 2004

INDEX OF FIRST LINES

32 什么事都可能发生。你知道朱庇特

གང་རུང་འབྱུང་བ་ཡིས། ཁྱེད་ཀྱིས་རྟོགས།

34 何が起きたって不思議じゃないんだ。
Apa-apa boleh terjadi. Anda kan tahu...

36 Tout peut arriver. Souviens-toi de Jupiter
Chochote chaweza kutokea. Wajua Jupita...

38 De todo puede suceder. ¿Ya sabéis cómo...
Denetik gerta daiteke. Badakizue Jupiterrek

40 कुछ भी हो सकता है, कैसे वृहस्पति अपनी
کچھ بھی ہو سکتا ہے۔ تمہیں معلوم ہے کہ کیسے رومی دیوتا جو پٹر

42 Her şey olabilir. Tanrılar Kralı Jupiter'in
Όλα μπορούν να συμβούν. Ξέρεις πως ο Δίας